KETO

BREAD MACHINE

COOKBOOK

EASY KETOGENIC RECIPES
FOR BAKING HOMEMADE BREAD

Sharon Basiar

HAPPINESS IS SMELL OF FRESHLY BAKED BREAD

TABLE OF CONTENTS

INTRODUCTION

The nutrients you consume are divided into two essential groups, namely macronutrients and micronutrients. Macronutrients are, for example, carbohydrates, proteins, and fats, while micronutrients are minerals and vitamins found in the food we eat.

Micronutrients

One difference between micronutrients and macronutrients is the amount needed to be consumed. While you will need to consume more macronutrients, the same cannot be said about micronutrients, which must be consumed in fewer amounts. Still, this does not mean that micronutrients are less important. Actually, they are very important in order to help the body function well. Micronutrients play a role in helping to regulate the energy levels in the body, maintain a healthy metabolic rate, and maintain healthy cell function, as well as general health and well-being of the whole body.

Macronutrients

Macronutrients are essentially those foods that we consume in order to supply our bodies with the energy we need to survive. These foods consist of three types, mainly proteins, fats, and carbohydrates. These nutrients are needed in substantial amounts by the body in order for it to function well and to grow and develop, too. Each food type delivers a certain amount of macronutrients to the body and whether these macronutrients are healthy or not is dependent on what you consume.

Fats can be scary when you first hear of them. But do not be afraid. The fatty foods mentioned here are healthy fats, which are a necessary part of your daily food intake. These fats are vital in the development of brain functionality, cell growth, and development, as well as enabling the body to break down and absorb vitamins. Foods that are a source of healthy fats include seeds like pumpkin seeds, flax seeds, and chia seeds; nuts like groundnuts, walnuts, almonds, and peanuts; and fruits like olives, avocados, etc.

Carbohydrates are the body's main source of glucose, which is obtained by breaking down the sugars contained in them.

Protein is very important to the general functionality of your body. From the repairs needed to a healthy immune system and cell regeneration, proteins play a very vital role.

Benefits of the Keto Diet to Your Health

You achieve reduced amounts of glucose and blood sugar levels in the body, especially for diabetes patients. This is because of the state of ketosis that your body experiences, which means you have less glucose produced in the body. Studies have shown the reduction of blood glucose in the body known as hba1c— especially for patients suffering from type 2 diabetes. This reduction in blood glucose levels and the control attained as a result can— in the long run— help reduce the risk of complications.

You achieve weight loss. Keto diets enable you not only to lose weight but also to keep it healthy. For the body to be in a state of ketosis, fewer amounts of carbs must be consumed, which will result in weight loss, as well as increased and improved metabolic rate.

Yet another health benefit of keto diet is a healthier liver. This is due to the reduced amount of fats in the liver in the long run. Fat accumulation results in type 2 diabetes and fatty liver diseases, as well. Being in control of your levels of blood sugars due to the keto diet means reducing food cravings in general. Methods like intermittent fasting (if) can be used by those under the keto diet because they can generally go longer without consuming foods.

Risks Associated with the Keto Diets

Like everything else in life, keto diets also have their risks, which are important to know. These risks include the following:

Risk of Getting Kidney Stones

Developing kidney stones is a possible side effect of being on a ketogenic diet. Kidney stones are a result of consuming more animal protein, which— in the long run— results in your urine being more acidic, together with an increase in uric acid and calcium. This is the perfect setting for kidney stones formation. It is important to note that high uric acid in the body is also the main cause of gout. Therefore, the ketogenic diets are not recommended to those people with kidney problems.

For patients suffering from diabetes, they should proceed with caution while on the ketogenic diet, and preferably, they should have a constant follow-up with their doctor. This is because— as much as reduced and controlled blood sugar levels are beneficial— a significant drop can prove detrimental. Keto diets call for reduced carb intake, which means that less sugar is produced in the body, causing moments of hypoglycemia, and this is especially dangerous to patients with type 1 diabetes.

Another risk of being on the keto diet is dehydration. This is because of the less amount of carbs consumed, which means that less glucose is produced as well. Another risk is the loss of the number of electrolytes in the body, where the kidneys are forced to release more electrolytes because of the less amount of insulin available. This combination can result in the development of keto flu, which is characterized by headache, fatigue, nausea, cramps, and irritability, among other symptoms.

A reduction in the number of carbs consumed can result in a nutrient deficiency as well. The reason for this is that there is less and less fiber consumed. Potassium levels are also reduced due to the decrease in the number of starchy foods. Therefore, those on the keto diet need to make the conscious choice to always have more keto food types that can be a source of potassium, such as avocado, chia, and flaxseeds.

Keto has also been known to cause constipation. This is due to the restriction of fiber-rich foods. This leads to less laxation. It is also important to note that in the first few days or weeks on the keto diet, as the body adjusts, you may experience bouts of diarrhea. This is because the body is still adjusting to digesting large amounts of fats.

Keto diets can result in fast muscle loss. Loss of muscles can be detrimental, especially as you age. It can also result in reduced activity and an increase in the risk of falling.

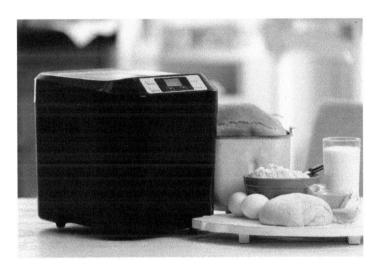

Get to Know Your Bread Machine

Take time to familiarize yourself with the machine. There should be a hinged lid that can be lifted and shut, a window to see into the pan, and a small vent. Next to the lid, there should be a control panel with the function buttons.

Inside the bread machine, you'll see a bread pan or bread bucket with a handle. It works as a mixing bowl and baking pan. There is a little bread paddle or kneading blade found at the center of the bucket. It should be removed once the baking is done. Both the bread bucket and blade are removable.

Familiarize Yourself with the Settings

The control panel contains the display screen and the function buttons. You might find these buttons:

- Select

- Stop/Start

- Crust Color

- Timer or Arrow

When you plug in the machine, it will automatically be on the default setting, which is the Basic button.

When you choose the Select button, you'll find several choice settings on what kind of bread you intend to make. The most common choices would be:

- White or Basic

- Whole Wheat

- French

- Pizza

- Multigrain

You will find a Bake mode option —Bake, Bake Rapid, Dough, and Sandwich. This button will determine the sequence of mixing, kneading, rising, and then baking. For instance, you chose the Dough mode. The machine will stop without cooking the dough. At this point, you will have to open the lid and remove the dough. After which you will take it out for reshaping and cooking in the oven.

You will simply press the Select button until you reach the desired setting.

There is also the size setting button —Small, Medium, Large, X-Large (sometimes it will also be in terms of loaf size, e.g., 1.5lb, 2lb).

You will also find the Crust setting (which is not available on every machine). If there is a Crust button in your machine, there will be three settings to choose from —Light, Medium, Dark. The machine will always start on the default setting, which is Medium. Normally, the Crust button won't work until you have selected the dough cycle and before you press the Start button.

When using the Timer button, refer to the recipe you want to follow. Once you've secured the bread bucket in the machine and you have closed the lid, you should select the cycle that is needed. You can use the Arrow buttons when adjusting the time on the display screen.

You'll press the Start button to start baking your bread.

You don't need to monitor the cooking time because you already set the timer and the cycle setting.

Recipes: Low-Carbohydrate Food

1. Coconut Bars

Preparation time: 10 minutes
Cooking time: 15 minutes
Servings: 6

Ingredients:

- 3 large eggs
- 1 teaspoon vanilla
- 2 cups shredded coconut
- ¼ cup almonds, chopped
- 1 tablespoon chia seeds
- 2 tablespoons swerve
- 2 tablespoons almond butter
- ½ cup of coconut oil
- ¼ cup flaxseed meal
- Pinch of salt

Directions:

1. Pour 2 cups of water into the instant pot, then place a trivet in the pot.
2. Line a baking pan with parchment paper and set it aside.
3. Add all ingredients into the large mixing bowl and mix until the mixture is sticky.
4. Add the mixture to the prepared baking pan and spread evenly with the palms of your hands.
5. Cover baking pan with foil and place on top of the trivet in the instant pot.
6. Seal pot with the lid and select manual and set timer for 15 minutes.
7. Release pressure using the quick-release method, then open the lid.

8. Cut the bar into slices and place in the refrigerator for 1-2 hours.

Nutrition:

- Calories: 376
- Fat: 36.4 g
- Carbohydrates: 8.4 g
- Protein: 7.2 g

2. Chia Nut Bars

Preparation time: 10 minutes
Cooking time: 25 minutes
Servings: 10

Ingredients:

- 1 cup almond butter
- 2 ½ tablespoons swerve
- 2 tablespoons chia seeds
- ¼ teaspoon cinnamon
- ½ cup almond flour
- ¼ cup unsweetened cocoa powder
- ¼ cup hazelnuts, chopped
- 1 cup almonds, chopped
- Pinch of salt

Directions:

1. Line a baking dish with parchment paper and set it aside.
2. Pour 1 cup of water into the instant pot and place trivet in the pot.
3. Add the almond butter, swerve, cinnamon, almond flour, cocoa powder, hazelnuts, almonds, and salt into the food processor and process until smooth.
4. Transfer mixture into the large bowl. Add chia seeds and mix well.
5. Transfer mixture into the prepared baking dish and spread mixture evenly.
6. Cover baking dish with foil and place on top of the trivet in the instant pot.
7. Seal pot with the lid and select manual and set timer for 15 minutes.

8. Allow releasing pressure naturally for 10 minutes, then release using the Quick release method.

9. Open the lid carefully. Remove the baking dish from the instant pot and let it cool for 20 minutes.

10. Cut the bar into slices and serve.

Nutrition:

- •Calories. 122
- •Fat: 10.3 g
- •Carbohydrates: 5.9 g
- •Protein: 4.6 g

3. Chocolate Cheesecake

Preparation time: 10 minutes
Cooking time: 35 minutes
Servings: 6

Ingredients:

- 16 oz cream cheese
- 2 large eggs
- 4 tablespoons unsweetened cocoa powder
- 2 tablespoons heavy whipping cream
- ½ teaspoon vanilla
- 2 teaspoons coconut flour
- ½ cup Swerve

For topping:

- 2 teaspoons swerve
- ½ cup sour cream

Directions:

1. Grease spring-form pan with butter and line with parchment paper. Set aside.
2. Add cream cheese, cocoa powder, whipping cream, vanilla, coconut flour, and swerve into the large bowl and mix until well combined using a hand mixer.
3. Add eggs one at a time and mix until well combined.
4. Pour cheesecake batter into the prepared pan.
5. Pour 1 ½ cups of water into the instant pot, then place a trivet in the pot.
6. Place cake pan on top of the trivet.

7. Seal pot with the lid and cook on manual high pressure for 35 minutes.

8. Allow releasing pressure naturally and then open the lid. Remove the cake pan from the pot and let it cool completely.

9. Mix together the topping ingredients and spread them on top of the cake.

10. Place cake in the refrigerator for 3-4 hours.

11. Slice and serve.

Nutrition:

- Calories: 376
- Fat: 35.1 g
- Carbohydrates: 7.9 g
- Protein: 9.9 g

GLUTEN
FREE
RECIPES

4. Pull-Apart Bread Rolls

Preparation time: 2 hours
Cooking time: 15 minutes
Servings: 8

Ingredients:

- 2 cups almond flour
- 3 tablespoons psyllium husk powder
- 2 teaspoons baking powder
- 3 tablespoons whey protein powder
- 2 teaspoons insulin
- 2 teaspoons active dry yeast
- 2 egg whites

- 2 eggs
- ¼ cup butter
- 1/3 cup lukewarm water
- ¼ cup Greek yoghurt

Directions:

1. Add all ingredients to the Bread Machine.

2. Select Dough setting. When the time is over, transfer the dough to the floured surface. Shape it into a ball and then cut it into about 8 even pieces.

3. Line a pie dish with parchment paper. Form 8 dough balls. Cover the dish with greased cling film and let them sit for 60 minutes in a warm place.

4. Heat the oven to 350°F and bake for 15 minutes. Cover with foil and bake for 10 more minutes.

Nutrition:

- Calories: 257
- Fat: 20.1g
- Total carbohydrates: 7.1 g
- Protein: 12.4 g

5. Fluffy Paleo Bread

Preparation time: 10 minutes
Cooking time: 40 minutes
Servings: 15

Ingredients:

- 1 ¼ cup almond flour
- 5 eggs
- 1 teaspoon lemon juice
- 1/3 cup avocado oil
- 1 dash black pepper
- ½ teaspoon sea salt
- 3 to 4 tablespoons tapioca flour
- 1 to 2 teaspoons poppy seed
- ¼ cup ground flaxseed

- ½ teaspoon baking soda

Top with:

- Poppy seeds
- Pumpkin seeds

Directions:

1. Preheat the oven to 350°F.
2. Line a baking pan with parchment paper and set it aside.
3. In a bowl, add eggs, avocado oil, and lemon juice and whisk until combined.
4. In another bowl, add tapioca flour, almond flour, baking soda, flaxseed, black pepper, and poppy seed. Mix.
5. Add the lemon juice mixture into the flour mixture and mix well.
6. Add the batter into the prepared loaf pan and top with extra pumpkin seeds and poppy seeds.
7. Cover loaf pan and transfer into the prepared oven.
8. Bake for 20 minutes. Remove cover and bake until an inserted knife comes out clean—after about 15 to 20 minutes.
9. Remove from oven and cool.
10. Slice and serve.

Nutrition:

- Calories: 149
- Fat: 12.9 g
- Carbohydrates: 4.4 g
- Protein: 5 g

6. Spicy Bread

Preparation time: 10 minutes
Cooking time: 40 minutes
Servings: 6

Ingredients:

- ½ cup coconut flour
- 6 eggs
- 3 large jalapenos, sliced
- 4 ounces turkey bacon, sliced
- ½ cup ghee
- ¼ teaspoon baking soda
- ¼ teaspoon salt
- ¼ cup water

Directions:

1. Preheat the oven to 400°F.
2. Cut bacon and jalapenos on a baking tray and roast for 10 minutes.
3. Flip and bake for 5 more minutes.
4. Remove seeds from the jalapenos.
5. Place jalapenos and bacon slices in a food processor and blend until smooth.
6. In a bowl, add ghee, eggs, and ¼-cup water. Mix well.
7. Then add the coconut flour, baking soda, and salt. Stir to mix.
8. Add bacon and jalapeno mix.
9. Grease the loaf pan with ghee.
10. Pour batter into the loaf pan.
11. Bake for 40 minutes.
12. Enjoy.

Nutrition:

- Calories: 240
- Fat: 20 g
- Carbohydrates: 5 g
- Protein: 9 g

7. Moist Mango Bread

Preparation time: 30 minutes
Cooking time: 55-60 minutes
Servings: 8-10 slices

Ingredients:

- 2 cups almond flour, finely ground
- 1/2 cup semi-sweet chocolate chips
- 2-3 ripe mangoes
- 1 1/4 cup toasted macadamia nuts/pecans, coarsely chopped
- 3/8 cup unsalted butter, melted
- 1/4 cup sweetener: xylitol or a combination of 1/4 cup erythritol and 1/4 cup xylitol
- 3 large eggs, lightly beaten
- 1 tablespoon baking powder
- 4 tablespoons plain full-fat yogurt or coconut milk
- 1 teaspoon baking soda
- 1 teaspoon vanilla extract

Directions:

1. Add all ingredients to the Bread Machine.
2. Select Dough setting and press Start. Mix the ingredients for about 4-5 minutes. After that press the Stop button.
3. Smooth out the top of the loaf. Choose Bake mode and press Start. Let it bake for about 55 minutes.
4. Remove bread from the bread machine and let it rest for 10 minutes. Enjoy!

Nutrition:

- Calories: 380   Fat: 11 g
- Total carbs: 46 g   Protein: 5 g

8. Keto Fluffy Cloud Bread

Preparation time: 25 minutes
Cooking time: 25 minutes
Servings: 3

Ingredients:

- 1 pinch salt
- ½ tablespoon ground psyllium husk powder
- ½ tablespoon baking powder
- ¼ teaspoon cream of tarter
- 2 eggs, separated
- ½ cup, cream cheese

Directions:

1. Preheat the oven to 300°F and line a baking tray with parchment paper.
2. Whisk egg whites in a bowl until soft peaks are formed.
3. Mix egg yolks with cream cheese, salt, cream of tartar, psyllium husk powder, and baking powder in a bowl.
4. Add the egg whites carefully and transfer to the baking tray.
5. Place in the oven and bake for 25 minutes.
6. Remove from the oven and serve.

Nutrition:

- Calories: 185
- Fat: 16.4 g
- Carbohydrates: 3.9 g
- Protein: 6.6 g

9. Keto Yeast Loaf Bread

Preparation time: 5 minutes
Cooking time: 4 hours
Servings: 16 slices (1 slice per serving)

Ingredients:

- 1 package dry yeast
- ½ teaspoon sugar
- 1 1/8 cup warm water about 90-100 ° F
- 3 tablespoons olive oil or avocado oil
- 1 cup vital wheat gluten flour
- ¼ cup oat flour
- ¾ cup soy flour
- ¼ cup flax meal
- ¼ cup wheat bran course, unprocessed
- 1 tablespoon sugar
- 1 ½ teaspoon baking powder
- 1 teaspoon salt

Directions:

1. Mix the sugar, water, and yeast in the bread bucket to try the yeast. If the yeast does not bubble, toss and replace it.

2. Combine all the dry ingredients in a bowl and mix thoroughly. Pour over the wet ingredients in the bread bucket.

3. Set the bread machine and select Basis cycle to bake the loaf. Close the lid. This takes 3 to 4 hours.

4. When the cycle ends, remove the bread from the bread machine.

5. Cool on a rack before slicing.

6. Serve with butter or light jam.

Nutrition:

- Calories: 99
- Calories from fat: 45
- Total Fat: 5 g
- Total Carbohydrates: 7 g
- Net Carbohydrates: 5 g
- Protein: 9 g

10. Protein Keto Bread

Preparation time: 10 minutes
Cooking time: 40 minutes
Servings: 12

Ingredients:

- 1/2 cup unflavored protein powder
- 6 tablespoons almond flour
- 5 pastured eggs, separated
- 1 tablespoon coconut oil
- 1 teaspoon baking powder
- 1 teaspoon xanthan gum
- 1 pinch Himalayan pink salt
- 1 pinch stevia (optional)

Direction:

1. Start by preheating the oven to 325 °F.
2. Grease a ceramic loaf dish with coconut oil and layer it with parchment paper.
3. Add egg whites to a bowl and beat well until it forms peaks.
4. In a separate bowl, mix the dry ingredients together.
5. Mix wet ingredients in another bowl and beat well.
6. Add dry mixture and mix well until smooth.
7. Add the egg whites and mix evenly.
8. Spread the bread batter in the prepared loaf pan.
9. Bake the bread for 40 minutes or until it's done.
10. Slice into 12 slices and serve.

Nutrition:

- Calories: 165
- Total Fat: 14 g
- Saturated Fat: 7 g
- Total Carbohydrates: 6 g
- Fiber: 3 g
- Protein: 5 g

11.Hawaiian Dinner Bread

Preparation time: 10 minutes
Cooking time: 29 minutes
Servings: 10

Ingredients:

- 1 ½ cups almond flour
- 2 teaspoons baking powder
- 3/4 cup powdered Swerve
- 3 cups mozzarella cheese, shredded
- 3 ounces cream cheese
- 2 eggs
- 6 drops avocado oil
- 1 teaspoon fresh ginger paste

Directions:

1. Start by adding almond flour, Swerve, and baking powder to a medium-size bowl and mix together.
2. In a separate bowl, add cream cheese and mozzarella cheese and heat for 1 minute in a microwave until melted.
3. Mix well and pour this mixture into the dry mixture.
4. Whisk well, then add ginger, oil, and eggs.
5. Beat well to make a smooth, sticky dough.
6. Cut the dough into 10 equal parts.
7. Roll each piece into a ball and place them in a greased baking pan.
8. Bake them for 29 minutes or until golden brown.
9. Serve warm.

Nutrition:

- Calories: 151
- Total Fat: 12.2 g
- Saturated Fat: 2.4 g
- Cholesterol: 110 mg
- Sodium: 276 mg
- Total Carbohydrates: 3.2 g
- Fiber: 1.9 g
- Sugar: 0.4 g
- Protein: 8.8 g

12. Keto Almond Bread

Preparation time: 10 minutes
Cooking time: 55 min
Servings: 7

Ingredients:

- ½ cup spread
- 2 tablespoons coconut oil
- 7 eggs
- 2 cups almond flour

Directions:

1. Preheat the broiler to 355 °F.
2. Line a portion container with material paper.
3. Blend the eggs in a bowl on high for as long as two minutes.
4. Add the almond flour, liquefied coconut oil, and dissolved spread to the eggs. Keep on blending.
5. Scratch the blend into the portion container.
6. Heat for 45-50 minutes or until a toothpick comes out clean.

Nutrition:

- Calories: 21 g
- Fat: 4.7 g
- Carbohydrates: 44.2 g
- Protein: 0 g

13. Olive Keto Bread

Preparation time: 10 minutes
Cooking time: 25 minutes
Servings: 8

Ingredients:

- 3 tablespoons olive oil
- 2 garlic cloves, smashed
- 1¼ cups blanched almond flour
- 1 tablespoon coconut flour
- 2 teaspoons lemon zest
- 2 teaspoons baking powder
- 2 teaspoons Za'atar, divided
- ¼ teaspoon sea salt
- 1 tablespoon apple cider vinegar
- 3 large egg whites
- ½ cup shredded Mozzarella cheese
- ¼ cup Kalamata olives, pitted, chopped
- ½ cup grated Parmesan cheese

Directions:

1. Start by preheating the oven at 400 °F. Then grease a 9-inch loaf pan.
2. Put a suitable skillet over low heat and add oil and garlic to sauté for 4 minutes. Remove the garlic from the oil.
3. Whisk almond flour with lemon zest, coconut flour, baking powder, salt, and a teaspoon of Za'atar in a large bowl.
4. Mix 3 tablespoons of warm water with vinegar in a separate small bowl.
5. Beat egg whites until foamy using a hand mixer.
6. Add vinegar mixture, dry mixture, and 2 tablespoons garlic oil.

7. Mix well and add olives and mozzarella.

8. Make a smooth dough and keep it aside.

9. Mix 1 teaspoon Za'atar and Parmesan in a medium bowl.

10. Roll the dough into the Parmesan mixture and then divide the dough into small pieces.

11. Place the pieces on the baking sheet and bake for 20 minutes until golden.

12. Serve fresh.

Nutrition:

- Calories: 267
- Total Fat: 24.5 g
- Saturated Fat: 17.4 g
- Cholesterol: 153 mg
- Sodium: 217 mg
- Total Carbohydrates: 8.4 g
- Sugar: 2.3 g
- Fiber: 1.3 g
- Protein: 3.1 g

14. Keto Blueberry Bread

Preparation time: 10 minutes
Cooking time: 50 minutes
Servings: 8

Ingredients:

- 5 medium eggs
- 2 cups almond flour
- 2 tablespoons coconut flour
- 1/2 cup blueberries
- 1 1/2 teaspoons baking powder
- 3 tablespoons heavy whipping cream
- 1/2 cup erythritol
- 3 tablespoons butter softened
- 1 teaspoon vanilla extract

Directions:

1. Start by preheating the oven to 350 °F. Then, line a 9x 5-inch loaf pan with parchment paper and butter.
2. Whisk eggs with vanilla extract and sweetener in a large bowl using a hand mixer.
3. Once it's frothy, add whipping cream and mix well.
4. Separately, mix the dry and wet ingredients in two bowls, then whisk them together.
5. Add butter and beat well, then add the berries.
6. Evenly spread the batter in the loaf pan and bake for 50 minutes until golden brown.
7. Slice and serve.

Nutrition:

- Calories: 201
- Total Fa: 2.2 g
- Saturated Fat: 2.4 g
- Total Carbohydrates: 4.3 g
- Fiber: 0.9 g
- Protein: 8.8 g

KETO HERB, SPICY and SEEDED LOAVES

15. Herbed Garlic Bread

Preparation time: 10 minutes
Cooking time: 45 minutes
Servings: 10

Ingredients:

- ½ cup coconut flour
- 8 tablespoons melted butter, cooled
- teaspoon baking powder
- 6 large eggs
- 1 teaspoon garlic powder
- 1 teaspoon rosemary, dried
- ¼ teaspoon salt
- ½ teaspoon onion powder

Directions:

1. Prepare bread machine loaf pan, greasing it with cooking spray.
2. In a bowl, add coconut flour, baking powder, onion, garlic, rosemary, and salt into a bowl. Combine and mix well.
3. In another bowl, add eggs, and beat until bubbly on top.
4. Add melted butter into the bowl with the eggs and beat until mixed.
5. Following the instructions on your machine's manual, mix the dry ingredients into the wet ingredients and pour in the bread machine loaf pan, taking care to follow how to mix in the baking powder.
6. Place the bread pan in the machine, and select the Basic bread setting, together with the bread size and crust type, if available, then press start once you have closed the lid of the machine.
7. When the bread is ready, using oven mitts, remove the bread pan from the machine.

8. Let it cool before slicing.
9. Cool, slice, and enjoy.

Nutrition:

- Calories: 147
- Fat: 12.5 g
- Carbohydrates: 3.5 g
- Protein: 4.6 g

16. Flax Seed Bread

Preparation time: *10 minutes*
Cooking time: *20 minutes*
Servings: *6*
Ingredients:

- 2 cups flax seed, ground
- 1 tablespoon baking powder
- 1 ½ cups protein isolate
- A pinch of salt
- 6 egg whites, whisked
- 1 egg, whisked
- ¾ cup water
- 3 tablespoons coconut oil, melted
- ¼ cup stevia

Directions:

1. In a bowl, mix all dry ingredients and stir well.
2. In a separate bowl, mix the egg whites and the rest of the wet ingredients, stir well and combine the 2 mixtures.
3. Stir the bread and mix well. Pour into a loaf pan and bake at 350 °F for 20 minutes.
4. Cool the bread down, slice, and serve.

Nutrition:

- Calories: 263
- Fat: 17 g
- Fiber: 4 g
- Carbohydrates: 2 g
- Protein 20 g

17. Keto Spinach Bread

Preparation time: 10 minutes
Cooking time: 30 minutes
Servings: 10

Ingredients:

- ½ cup spinach, chopped
- 1 tablespoon olive oil
- 1 cup water
- 3 cups almond flour
- A pinch of salt and black pepper
- 1 tablespoon stevia
- 1 teaspoon baking powder
- 1 teaspoon baking soda
- ½ cup cheddar, shredded

Directions:

1. In a bowl, mix the flour, with salt, pepper, stevia, baking powder, baking soda, and Cheddar and stir well.
2. Add the remaining ingredients, stir the batter really well and pour it into a lined loaf pan.
3. Cook at 350 °F for 30 minutes, cool the bread down, slice, and serve.

Nutrition:

- Calories: 142
- Fat: 7 g
- Fiber: 3 g
- Carbohydrates: 5 g
- Protein: 6 g

18. Cinnamon Asparagus Bread

Preparation time: 10 minutes
Cooking time: 45 minutes
Servings: 8

Ingredients:

- 1 cup stevia
- ¾ cup coconut oil, melted
- 1 and ½ cups almond flour
- 2 eggs, whisked
- A pinch of salt
- 1 teaspoon baking soda
- 1 teaspoon cinnamon powder
- 2 cups asparagus, chopped
- Cooking spray

Directions:

1. In a bowl, mix all the ingredients except the cooking spray and stir the batter really well.
2. Pour this batter into a loaf pan greased with cooking spray and bake at 350 °F for 45 minutes, cool the bread down, slice, and serve.

Nutrition:

- Calories: 165
- Fat: 6 g
- Fiber: 3 g
- Carbohydrates: 5 g
- Protein: 6 g

19. Kale and Cheese Bread

Preparation time: 10 minutes
Cooking time: 1 hour
Servings: 8
Ingredients:

- 2 cups kale, chopped
- 1 cup warm water
- 1 teaspoon baking powder
- 1 teaspoon baking soda
- 2 tablespoons olive oil
- 2 teaspoons stevia
- 1 cup Parmesan, grated
- 3 cups almond flour
- A pinch of salt
- 1 egg
- 2 tablespoons basil, chopped

Directions:

1. In a bowl, mix the flour, salt, Parmesan, stevia, baking soda, and baking powder and stir.
2. Add the rest of the ingredients gradually and stir the dough well.
3. Transfer it to a lined loaf pan, cook at 350 °F for 1 hour, cool down, slice, and serve.

Nutrition:

- Calories: 231
- Fat: 7 g
- Fiber: 2 g
- Carbohydrates: 5 g
- Protein: 7 g

20. Beed Bread

Preparation time: 1 hour and 10 minutes
Cooking time: 35 minutes
Servings: 6

Ingredients:

- 1 cup warm water
- 3 and ½ cups almond flour
- 1 and ½ cups beet puree
- 2 tablespoons olive oil
- A pinch of salt
- 1 teaspoon stevia
- 1 teaspoon baking powder
- 1 teaspoon baking soda

Directions:

- In a bowl, mix the flour with the water and beet puree and stir well.
- Add the rest of the ingredients, stir the dough well and pour it into a lined loaf pan.
- Leave the mix to rise in a warm place for 1 hour, and then bake the bread at 375 °F for 35 minutes.
- Cool the bread down, slice, and serve.

Nutrition:

- Calories: 200
- Fat: 8 g
- Fiber: 3 g
- Carbohydrates: 5 g
- Protein: 6 g

21. Keto Celery Bread

Preparation time: 2 hours and 10 minutes
Cooking time: 35 minutes
Servings: 6

Ingredients:

- ½ cup celery, chopped
- 3 cups almond flour
- 1 teaspoon baking powder
- 1 teaspoon baking soda
- A pinch of salt
- 2 tablespoons coconut oil, melted
- ½ cup celery puree

Directions:

1. In a bowl, mix the flour with salt, baking powder, and baking soda and stir.
2. Add the rest of the ingredients, stir the dough well, cover the bowl and keep in a warm place for 2 hours.
3. Transfer the dough to a lined loaf pan and cook at 400 °F for 35 minutes.
4. Cool the bread down, slice, and serve.

Nutrition:

- Calories: 162
- Fat: 6 g
- Fiber: 2 g
- Carbohydrates: 6 g
- Protein: 4 g

22. Easy Cucumber Bread

Preparation time: 10 minutes
Cooking time: 50 minutes
Servings: 6

Ingredients:

- 1 cup erythritol
- 1 cup coconut oil, melted
- 1 cup almonds, chopped
- 1 teaspoon vanilla extract
- A pinch of salt
- A pinch of nutmeg, ground
- ½ teaspoon baking powder
- A pinch of cloves
- 3 eggs
- 1 teaspoon baking soda
- 1 tablespoon cinnamon powder
- 2 cups cucumber, peeled, deseeded, and shredded
- 3 cups coconut flour
- Cooking spray

Directions:

1. In a bowl, mix the flour with cucumber, cinnamon, baking soda, cloves, baking powder, nutmeg, salt, vanilla extract, and the almonds and stir well.
2. Add the rest of the ingredients except the coconut flour, stir well and transfer the dough to a loaf pan greased with cooking spray.
3. Bake at 325 °F for 50 minutes, cool the bread down, slice, and serve.

Nutrition:

- Calories: 243
- Fat: 12 g
- Fiber: 3 g
- Carbohydrates: 6 g
- Protein: 7 g

23. Red Bell Pepper Bread

Preparation time: 10 minutes
Cooking time: 30 minutes
Servings: 12

Ingredients:

- 1 and ½ cups red bell peppers, chopped
- 1 teaspoon baking powder
- 1 teaspoon baking soda
- 2 tablespoons warm water
- 1 and ¼ cups Parmesan, grated
- A pinch of salt
- 4 cups almond flour
- 2 tablespoons ghee, melted
- 1/3 cup almond milk
- 1 egg

Directions:

1. In a bowl, mix the flour with salt, Parmesan, baking powder, baking soda, and bell peppers and stir well.
2. Add the rest of the ingredients and stir the bread batter well.
3. Transfer it to a lined loaf pan and bake at 350 °F for 30 minutes.
4. Cool the bread down, slice, and serve.

Nutrition:

- Calories: 100
- Fat: 5 g
- Fiber: 1 g
- Carbohydrates: 4 g
- Protein: 4 g

24. Tomato Bread

Preparation time: 1 hour and 10 minutes
Cooking time: 35 minutes
Servings: 12

Ingredients:

- 6 cups almond flour
- ½ teaspoon basil, dried
- ¼ teaspoon rosemary, dried
- 1 teaspoon oregano, dried
- ½ teaspoon garlic powder
- 2 tablespoons olive oil
- 2 cups tomato juice
- ½ cup tomato sauce
- 1 teaspoon baking powder
- 1 teaspoon baking soda
- 3 tablespoons swerve

Directions:

1. In a bowl, mix the flour with basil, rosemary, oregano, and garlic and stir.
2. Add the rest of the ingredients and stir the batter well.
3. Pour into a lined loaf pan, cover, and keep in a warm place for 1 hour.
4. Bake the bread at 375 °F for 35 minutes, cool down, slice, and serve.

Nutrition:

- Calories: 102
- Fat: 5 g
- Fiber: 3 g
- Carbohydrates: 7 g
- Protein: 4 g

25. Herbed Keto Bread

Preparation time: 1 hour and 30 minutes
Cooking time: 40 minutes
Servings: 8

Ingredients:

- 3 cups coconut flour
- 1 teaspoon baking powder
- 1 teaspoon baking soda
- 2 teaspoons stevia
- 1 ½ cups warm water
- ½ teaspoon basil, dried
- 1 teaspoon oregano, dried
- ½ teaspoon thyme, dried
- ½ teaspoon marjoram, dried
- 2 tablespoons olive oil

Directions:

1. In a bowl, mix the flour with baking powder, baking soda, stevia, basil, oregano, thyme, and marjoram and stir.
2. Add the remaining ingredients, mix the dough, cover and keep in a warm place for 1 hour and 30 minutes.
3. Transfer the dough to a floured working surface and knead it again for 2-3 minutes.
4. Transfer to a lined loaf pan and bake at 400 °F for 40 minutes.
5. Cool the bread down before serving.

Nutrition:
- Calories: 200
- Fat: 7 g
- Fiber: 3 g
- Carbohydrates: 5 g
- Protein: 6 g

26. Green Olive Bread

Preparation time: 10 minutes
Cooking time: 45 minutes
Servings: 10

Ingredients:

- 3 cups almond flour
- A pinch of salt
- ½ teaspoon baking powder
- 1 ½ cups warm water
- 3 tablespoons rosemary, chopped
- ½ cup green olives, pitted and chopped
- A pinch of salt and black pepper

Directions:

1. In a bowl, mix the flour with salt, rosemary, and baking powder and stir.
2. Add the rest of the ingredients, mix the dough well and transfer it to a lined loaf pan.
3. Bake at 400 °F for 45 minutes, cool down, slice, and serve.

Nutrition:

- Calories: 204
- Fat: 12 g
- Fiber: 4 g
- Carbohydrates: 5 g
- Protein: 7 g

27. Delicious Eggplant Bread

Preparation time: 10 minutes
Cooking time: 1 hour
Servings: 12

Ingredients:

- 4 eggs, whisked
- 1 cup erythritol
- ½ cup ghee, melted
- ½ cup coconut oil, melted
- 2 cups eggplant, peeled and grated
- 1 tablespoon vanilla extract
- 2 cups almond flour
- 1 ½ teaspoon cinnamon powder
- ¼ teaspoon nutmeg, ground
- ½ teaspoon baking powder
- 1 teaspoon baking soda
- A pinch of salt
- ½ cup pine nuts
- Cooking spray

Directions:

1. In a bowl, mix the flour with cinnamon, nutmeg, baking powder, baking soda, salt, pine nuts, and vanilla and stir.
2. Add the rest of the ingredients except the cooking spray, mix the batter well and pour into a loaf pan greased with the cooking spray.
3. Cook at 350 °F for 1 hour, cool down, slice, and serve.

Nutrition:

- Calories: 200
- Fat: 7 g
- Fiber: 3 g
- Carbohydrates: 5 g
- Protein: 6 g

28. Great Blackberries Bread

Preparation time: 10 minutes
Cooking time: 1 hour
Servings: 10

Ingredients:

- 2 cups almond flour
- ½ cup stevia
- 1 ½ teaspoons baking powder
- 1 teaspoon baking soda
- 2 eggs, whisked
- 1 ½ cups almond flour
- ¼ cup ghee, melted
- 1 tablespoon vanilla extract
- 1 cup blackberries, mashed
- Cooking spray

Directions:

1. In a bowl, mix the flour with the baking powder, baking soda, stevia, vanilla, and blackberries and stir well.
2. Add the rest of the ingredients, stir the batter and pour it into a loaf pan greased with cooking spray.
3. Bake at 400 °F for 1 hour, cool down, slice, and serve.

Nutrition:

- Calories: 200
- Fat: 7 g
- Fiber: 3 g
- Carbohydrates: 5 g
- Protein: 7 g

29. Keto Raspberries Bread

Preparation time: 10 minutes
Cooking time: 50 minutes
Servings: 6
Ingredients:

- 2 cups almond flour
- 1 teaspoon baking soda
- ¾ cup erythritol
- A pinch of salt
- 1 egg
- ¾ cup coconut milk
- ¼ cup ghee, melted
- 2 cups raspberries
- 2 teaspoons vanilla extract
- ¼ cup coconut oil, melted

Directions:

1. In a bowl, mix the flour with the baking soda, erythritol, salt, vanilla, and raspberries and stir.
2. Add the rest of the ingredients gradually and mix the batter well.
3. Pour this into a lined loaf pan and bake at 350 °F for 50 minutes.
4. Cool the bread down, slice, and serve.

Nutrition:

- Calories: 200
- Fat: 7 g
- Fiber: 3 g
- Carbohydrates: 5 g
- Protein: 7 g

30. Simple Strawberry Bread

Preparation time: 10 minutes
Cooking time: 50 minutes
Servings: 8

Ingredients:

- 3 and ½ cups almond flour
- 2 cups strawberries, chopped
- 1 teaspoon baking soda
- 2 cups swerve
- 1 tablespoon cinnamon powder
- 4 eggs, whisked
- 1 ¼ cups coconut oil, melted
- Cooking spray

Directions:

1. In a bowl, mix the flour with baking soda, swerve, strawberries, and cinnamon, and stir.
2. Add the remaining ingredients, stir the batter and pour this into 2 loaf pans greased with cooking spray.
3. Bake at 350 °F for 50 minutes, cool the bread down, slice, and serve.

Nutrition:

- Calories: 221
- Fat: 7 g
- Fiber: 4 g
- Carbohydrates: 5 g
- Protein: 3 g

31. Great Plum Bread

Preparation time: 10 minutes
Cooking time: 50 minutes
Servings: 8

Ingredients:

- 1 cup plums, pitted and chopped
- 1½ cups coconut flour
- ¼ teaspoon baking soda
- ½ cup ghee, melted
- A pinch of salt
- 1¼ cups swerve
- ½ teaspoon vanilla extract
- 1/3 cup coconut cream
- 2 eggs, whisked

Directions:

1. In a bowl, mix the flour with baking soda, salt, swerve, and vanilla and stir.
2. In a separate bowl, mix the plums with the remaining ingredients and stir.
3. Combine the 2 mixtures and stir the batter well.
4. Pour into 2 lined loaf pans and bake at 350 °F for 50 minutes.
5. Cool the bread down, slice, and serve them.

Nutrition:

- Calories: 199
- Fat: 8 g
- Fiber: 3 g
- Carbohydrates: 6 g
- Protein: 4 g

KETO HERB
and SPICE
RECIPES

32. Herb Bread

Preparation Time: 1 hour 20 minutes
Cooking Time: 50 minutes (20+30 minutes)
Servings: 1 loaf
Ingredients:

- 3/4 to 7/8 cup milk
- 1 tablespoon sugar
- 1 teaspoon salt
- 1 tablespoon butter or margarine
- 1/3 cup chopped onion
- 2 cups bread flour
- 1/2 teaspoon dried dill
- 1/2 teaspoon dried basil
- 1/2 teaspoon dried rosemary
- 1 ½ teaspoons active dry yeast

Directions:

1. .Place all the Ingredients in the bread pan. Select medium crus then the rapid bake cycle. Press starts.

2. .After 5-10 minutes, observe the dough as it kneads, if you hear straining sounds in your machine or if the dough appears stiff and dry, add 1 tablespoon Liquid at a time until the dough becomes smooth, pliable, soft, and slightly tacky to the touch.

3. .Remove the bread from the pan after baking. Place on rack and allow to cool for 1 hour before slicing.

Nutrition:

- Calories: 165
- Fat: 5 g

- Carbohydrates: 13 g
- Protein: 2 g

33. Rosemary Bread

Preparation Time: 2 hours 10 minutes
Cooking Time: 50 minutes
Servings: 1 loaf
Ingredients:

- ¾ cup + 1 tablespoon water at 80 degrees F
- 1 2/3 tablespoons melted butter, cooled
- 1 ½ teaspoons sugar
- 1 teaspoon salt
- 1 tablespoon fresh rosemary, chopped
- 2 cups white bread flour
- 1⅓ teaspoons instant yeast

Directions:

1. Add all of the ingredients to your bread machine, carefully following the instructions of the manufacturer.

2. Set the program of your bread machine to Basic/White Bread and set crust type to Medium.

3. Press START.

4. Wait until the cycle completes.

5. Once the loaf is ready, take the bucket out and let the loaf cool for 5 minutes.

6. Gently shake the bucket to remove the loaf.

7. Transfer to a cooling rack, slice, and serve.

Nutrition:

- Calories: 152
- Fat: 3 g
- Carbohydrates: 25 g
- Protein: 4 g
- Fiber: 1 g

34. Original Italian Herb Bread

Preparation Time: 2 hours 40 minutes
Cooking Time: 50 minutes
Servings: 2 loaves

Ingredients:

- 1 cup water at 80 degrees F
- ½ cup olive brine
- 1½ tablespoons butter
- 1 tablespoons sugar
- 1 teaspoons salt
- 5⅓ cups flour
- 1 teaspoons bread machine yeast
- 20 olives, black/green
- 1½ teaspoons Italian herbs

Directions:

1. Cut olives into slices.

2. Add all of the ingredients to your bread machine (except olives), carefully following the instructions of the manufacturer.

3. Set the program of your bread machine to French bread and set crust type to Medium.

4. Press START.

5. Once the maker beeps, add olives.

6 Wait until the cycle completes.

7 Once the loaf is ready, take the bucket out and let the loaf cool for 5 minutes.

8 Gently shake the bucket to remove the loaf.

9 Transfer to a cooling rack, slice, and serve.

Nutrition:

- Calories: 286
- Fat: 7 g
- Carbohydrates: 61 g
- Protein: 10 g
- Fiber: 1 g

35. Lovely Aromatic Lavender Bread

Preparation Time: 2 hours 10 minutes
Cooking Time: 50 minutes
Servings: 1 loaf

Ingredients:

- ¾ cup milk at 80 degrees F
- 1 tablespoon melted butter, cooled
- 1 tablespoon sugar
- ¾ teaspoon salt
- 1 teaspoon fresh lavender flower, chopped
- ¼ teaspoon lemon zest
- ¼ teaspoon fresh thyme, chopped
- 1 cup white bread flour
- ¾ teaspoon instant yeast

Directions:

1. Add all of the ingredients to your bread machine
2. Set the program of your bread machine to Basic/White Bread and set crust type to Medium.
3. Press START.
4. Wait until the cycle completes.
5. Once the loaf is ready, take the bucket out and let the loaf cool for 5 minutes.
6. Gently shake the bucket to remove the loaf.
7. Transfer to a cooling rack, slice, and serve.

Nutrition:

- Calories: 144
- Fat: 2 g
- Carbohydrates: 27 g
- Protein: 4 g   Fiber: 1 g

36. Oregano Mozza-Cheese Bread

Preparation Time: 2 hours 50 minutes
Cooking Time: 50 minutes
Servings: 2 loaves

Ingredients:
- 1 cup (milk + egg) mixture
- ½ cup mozzarella cheese
- 2¼ cups flour
- ¾ cup whole grain flour
- 1 tablespoon sugar
- 1 teaspoon salt
- 1 teaspoon oregano
- 1½ teaspoons dry yeast

Directions:
1. Add all of the ingredients to your bread machine
2. Set the program of your bread machine to Basic/White Bread and set crust type to Dark.
3. Press START.
4. Wait until the cycle completes.
5. Once the loaf is ready, take the bucket out and let the loaf cool for 5 minutes.
6. Gently shake the bucket to remove the loaf.
7. Transfer to a cooling rack, slice, and serve.

Nutrition:
- Calories: 209
- Fat: 2.1 g
- Carbohydrates: 40 g
- Protein: 7.7 g
- Fiber: 1 g

37. Cumin Bread

Preparation Time: 3 hours 30 minutes
Cooking Time: 15 minutes
Servings: 8

Ingredients:
- 1 1/3 cups bread machine flour, sifted
- 1½ teaspoons kosher salt
- 1½ tablespoon sugar
- 1 tablespoon bread machine yeast
- 1¾ cups lukewarm water
- 1 tablespoon black cumin
- 1 tablespoon sunflower oil

Directions:
1. Place all the dry and liquid ingredients in the pan and follow the instructions for your bread machine.
2. Set the baking program to BASIC and the crust type to MEDIUM.
3. If the dough is too dense or too wet, adjust the amount of flour and liquid in the recipe.
4. When the program has ended, take the pan out of the bread machine and let it cool for 5 minutes.
5. Shake the loaf out of the pan. If necessary, use a spatula.
6. Wrap the bread with a kitchen towel and set it aside for an hour. Otherwise, you can cool it on a wire rack.

Nutrition:
- Calories: 368
- Total Carbohydrate: 63 g
- Cholesterol: 0 mg
- Total Fat: 6.5 g
- Protein: 9.5 g
- Sodium: 444 mg
- Sugar: 2.5 g

38. Saffron Tomato Bread

Preparation Time: 3 hours 30 minutes
Cooking Time: 15 minutes
Servings: 10

Ingredients:

- 1 teaspoon bread machine yeast
- 2½ cups wheat bread machine flour
- 1 tablespoon panifarin
- 1½ teaspoons kosher salt
- 1½ tablespoons white sugar
- 1 tablespoon extra-virgin olive oil
- 1 tablespoon tomatoes, dried and chopped
- 1 tablespoon tomato paste
- ½ cup firm cheese (cubes)
- ½ cup feta cheese
- 1 pinch saffron
- 1½ cups serum

Directions:

1. Five minutes before cooking, pour in dried tomatoes and 1 tablespoon of olive oil. Add the tomato paste and mix.

2. Place all the dry and liquid ingredients, except additives, in the pan and follow the instructions for your bread machine.

3. Pay particular attention to measuring the ingredients. Use a measuring cup, measuring spoon, and kitchen scales to do so.

4. Set the baking program to BASIC and the crust type to MEDIUM.

5. Add the additives after the beep or place them in the dispenser of the bread machine.

6. Shake the loaf out of the pan. If necessary, use a spatula.

7. Wrap the bread with a kitchen towel and set it aside for an hour. Otherwise, you can cool it on a wire rack.

Nutrition:

- Calories: 260
- Total Carbohydrates: 33 g
- Cholesterol: 20 g
- Total Fat: 9.2g
- Protein: 8.9 g
- Sodium: 611 mg
- Sugar: 5.2 g

39. Cracked Black Pepper Bread

Preparation Time: 3 hours 30 minutes
Cooking Time: 15 minutes
Servings: 8

Ingredients:

- ¾ cup water, at 80°F to 90°F
- 1 tablespoon melted butter, cooled
- 1 tablespoon sugar
- ¾ teaspoon salt
- 1 tablespoon skim milk powder
- 1 tablespoon minced chives
- ½ teaspoon garlic powder
- ½ teaspoon cracked black pepper
- 2 cups white bread flour
- ¾ teaspoon bread machine or instant yeast

Directions:

1. Place the ingredients in your bread machine as recommended by the manufacturer.
2. Program the machine for Basic/White bread, select light or medium crust, and press Start.
3. When the loaf is done, remove the bucket from the machine.
4. Let the loaf cool for 5 minutes.
5. Gently shake the bucket to remove the loaf, and turn it out onto a rack to cool.

Nutrition:

- Calories: 141
- Total Carbohydrates: 27 g
- Total Fat: 2g
- Protein: 4 g
- Sodium: 215 mg
- Fiber: 1 g

40. Spicy Cajun Bread

Preparation Time: 2 hours
Cooking Time: 15 minutes
Servings: 8

Ingredients:

- ¾ cup water, at 80°F to 90°F
- 1 tablespoon melted butter, cooled
- 1 teaspoon tomato paste
- 1 tablespoon sugar
- 1 teaspoon salt
- 2 tablespoons skim milk powder
- ½ tablespoon Cajun seasoning
- 1/8 teaspoon onion powder
- 2 cups white bread flour
- 1 teaspoon bread machine or instant yeast

Directions:

1. Place the ingredients in your bread machine as recommended by the manufacturer.

2. Program the machine for Basic/White bread, select light or medium crust, and press Start.

3. When the loaf is done, remove the bucket from the machine.

4. Let the loaf cool for 5 minutes.

5. Gently shake the bucket to remove the loaf, and turn it out onto a rack to cool.

Nutrition:

- Calories: 141
- Total Carbohydrate: 27 g
- Total Fat: 2g
- Protein: 4 g
- Sodium: 215 mg
- Fiber: 1 g

41. Anise Lemon Bread

Preparation Time: 2 hours
Cooking Time: 15 minutes
Servings: 8

Ingredients:

- 2/3 cup water, at 80°F to 90°F
- 1 egg, at room temperature
- 2 2/3 tablespoons butter, melted and cooled
- 2 2/3 tablespoons honey
- ⅓ teaspoon salt
- 2/3 teaspoon anise seed
- 2/3 teaspoon lemon zest
- 2 cups white bread flour
- 1⅓ teaspoons bread machine or instant yeast

Directions:

1 Place the ingredients in your bread machine as recommended by the manufacturer.

2 Program the machine for Basic/White bread, select light or medium crust, and press Start.

3 When the loaf is done, remove the bucket from the machine.

4 Let the loaf cool for 5 minutes.

5 Gently shake the bucket to remove the loaf, and turn it out onto a rack to cool.

Nutrition:

- Calories: 158
- Total Carbohydrates: 27 g
- Total Fat: 5g
- Protein: 4 g
- Sodium: 131 mg
- Fiber: 1 g

42. Cardamon Bread

Preparation Time: 2 hours
Cooking Time: 15 minutes
Servings: 8

Ingredients:

- ½ cup milk, at 80°F to 90°F
- 1 egg, at room temperature
- 1 teaspoon melted butter, cooled
- 1 teaspoon honey
- 2/3 teaspoon salt
- 2/3 teaspoon ground cardamom
- 2 cups white bread flour
- ¾ teaspoon bread machine or instant yeast

Directions:

1. Place the ingredients in your bread machine as recommended by the manufacturer.
2. Program the machine for Basic/White bread, select light or medium crust, and press Start.
3. When the loaf is done, remove the bucket from the machine.
4. Let the loaf cool for 5 minutes.
5. Gently shake the bucket to remove the loaf, and turn it out onto a rack to cool.

Nutrition:

- Calories: 149
- Total Carbohydrates: 29 g
- Total Fat: 2g
- Protein: 5 g
- Sodium: 211 mg
- Fiber: 1 g

43. Breakfast Bread

Preparation Time: 15 minutes
Cooking Time: 40 minutes
Servings: 16 slices
Ingredients:

- ½ teaspoon. Xanthan gum
- ½ teaspoon. salt
- 2 tablespoons coconut oil
- ½ cup butter, melted
- 1 teaspoon baking powder
- 2 cups of almond flour
- Seven eggs

Directions:

1. Preheat the oven to 355F.
2. Beat eggs in a bowl on high for 2 minutes.
3. Add coconut oil and butter to the eggs and continue to beat.
4. Line a pan with baking paper and then pour the beaten eggs.
5. Pour in the rest of the ingredients and mix until it becomes thick.
6. Bake until a toothpick comes out dry. It takes 40 to 45 minutes.

Nutrition:

- Calories: 234
- Fat: 23 g
- Carbohydrates: 1 g
- Protein: 7 g

44. Peanut Butter and Jelly Bread

Preparation Time: 2 hours
Cooking Time: 1 hour and 10 minutes
Servings: 1 loaf

Ingredients:

- 1 ½ tablespoons vegetable oil
- 1 cup of water
- ½ cup blackberry jelly
- ½ cup peanut butter
- 1 teaspoon salt
- 1 tablespoon white sugar
- 2 cups of bread flour
- 1 cup whole-wheat flour
- 1 ½ teaspoons active dry yeast

Directions:

1. Put everything in your bread machine pan.
2. Select the basic setting.
3. Press the start button.
4. Take out the pan when done and set it aside for 10 minutes.

Nutrition:

- Calories: 153
- Carbohydrates: 20 g
- Fat: 9 g
- Cholesterol: 0 mg
- Protein: 4 g
- Fiber: 2 g
- Sugar: 11 g
- Sodium: 244 mg
- Potassium: 120 mg

45. English Muffin Bread

Preparation Time: 5 minutes
Cooking Time: 3 hours 40 minutes
Servings: 14

Ingredients:

- 1 teaspoon vinegar
- 1/4 to 1/3 cup water
- 1 cup lukewarm milk
- 2 tablespoons butter or 2 tablespoon vegetable oil
- 1½ teaspoons salt
- 1½ teaspoons sugar
- ½ teaspoon baking powder
- 3½ cups unbleached all-purpose flour
- 2 ¼ teaspoons instant yeast

Directions:

1. Add each ingredient to the bread machine in the order and at the temperature recommended by your bread machine manufacturer.

2. Close the lid, select the basic bread, low crust setting on your bread machine, and press start.

3. When the bread machine has finished baking, remove the bread and put it on a cooling rack.

Nutrition:

- Carbohydrates: 13 g
- Fat: 1 g
- Protein: 2 g
- Calories: 162

46. Cranberry Orange Breakfast Bread

Preparation Time: 5 minutes
Cooking Time: 3 hours 10 minutes
Servings: 14

Ingredients:

- 1 1/8 cups orange juice
- 2 tablespoons vegetable oil
- 2 tablespoons honey
- 3 cups bread flour
- 1 tablespoon dry milk powder
- ½ teaspoon ground cinnamon
- ½ teaspoon ground allspice
- 1 teaspoon salt
- 1 (.25 ounce) package active dry yeast
- 1 tablespoon grated orange zest
- 1 cup sweetened dried cranberries
- 1/3 cup chopped walnuts

Directions:

1. Add each ingredient to the bread machine in the order and at the temperature recommended by your bread machine manufacturer.

2. Close the lid, select the basic bread, low crust setting on your bread machine, and press start.

3. Add the cranberries and chopped walnuts 5 to 10 minutes before the last kneading cycle ends.

4. When the bread machine has finished baking, remove the bread and put it on a cooling rack.

Nutrition:

- Carbohydrates: 29 g
- Fat: 2 g
- Protein: 9 g
- Calories: 156

47. Buttermilk Honey Bread

Preparation Time: 5 minutes
Cooking Time: 3 hours 45 minutes
Servings: 14

Ingredients:

- ½ cup water
- ¾ cup buttermilk
- ¼ cup honey
- 3 tablespoons butter, softened and cut into pieces
- 3 cups bread flour
- 1½ teaspoons salt
- 2¼ teaspoons yeast (or 1 package)

Directions:

1. Add each ingredient to the bread machine in the order and at the temperature recommended by your bread machine manufacturer.

2. Close the lid, select the basic bread, medium crust setting on your bread machine, and press start.

3. When the bread machine has finished baking, remove the bread and put it on a cooling rack.

Nutrition:

- Carbohydrates: 19 g
- Fat: 1 g
- Protein: 2 g
- Calories: 142

48. Whole Wheat Breakfast Bread

Preparation Time: 5 minutes
Cooking Time: 3 hours 45 minutes
Servings: 14

Ingredients:

- 3 cups white whole wheat flour
- ½ teaspoon salt
- 1 cup water
- ½ cup coconut oil, liquified
- 4 tablespoons honey
- 2½ teaspoons active dry yeast

Directions:

1. Add each ingredient to the bread machine in the order and at the temperature recommended by your bread machine manufacturer.

2. Close the lid, select the basic bread, medium crust setting on your bread machine, and press start.

3. When the bread machine has finished baking, remove the bread and put it on a cooling rack.

Nutrition:

- Carbohydrates: 11 g
- Fat: 3 g
- Protein: 1 g
- Calories: 150

49. Cinnamon-Raisin Bread

Preparation Time: 5 minutes
Cooking Time: 3 hours
Servings: 4

Ingredients:

- 1 cup water
- 2 tablespoons butter, softened
- 3 cups Gold Medal Better for Bread flour
- 3 tablespoons sugar
- 1½ teaspoons salt
- 1 teaspoon ground cinnamon
- 2½ teaspoons bread machine yeast
- ¾ cup raisins

Directions:

1. Add each ingredient except the raisins to the bread machine in the order and at the temperature recommended by your bread machine manufacturer.

2. Close the lid, select the sweet or basic bread, medium crust setting on your bread machine, and press start.

3. Add raisins 10 minutes before the last kneading cycle ends.

4. When the bread machine has finished baking, remove the bread and put it on a cooling rack.

Nutrition:

- Carbohydrates: 38 g
- Fat: 2 g
- Protein: 4 g
- Calories: 180

50. Butter Bread Rolls

Preparation Time: 50 minutes
Cooking Time: 45 minutes
Servings: 24 rolls

Ingredients:
- 1 cup warm milk
- 1/2 cup butter or 1/2 cup margarine, softened
- 1/4 cup sugar
- 2 eggs
- 1 ½ teaspoons salt
- 4 cups bread flour
- 2 ¼ teaspoons active dry yeast

Directions:
1. In the bread machine pan, put all ingredients in the order suggested by the manufacturer.
2. Select dough setting.
3. When the cycle is completed, turn the dough onto a lightly floured surface.
4. Divide dough into 24 portions.
5. Shape dough into balls.
6. Place in a greased 13 inch by a 9-inch baking pan.
7. Cover and let rise in a warm place for 30-45 minutes.
8. Bake at 350 degrees for 13-16 minutes or until golden brown.

Nutrition:
- Carbohydrates: 38 g
- Fat: 2 g
- Protein: 4 g
- Calories: 180

KEEP
CALM
and
BAKE
BREAD

Conclusion

Focus your mindset toward the positive. Through a Keto diet, you can help prevent diabetes, heart diseases, and respiratory problems. If you already suffer from any of these, a Keto diet under a doctor's supervision can greatly improve your condition.

This book has introduced you to some of the easiest and delicious Keto bread recipes you can find. One of the most common struggles for anyone following the Keto diet is that they have to cut out so many of the foods they love, like sugary foods and starchy bread products. This book helps you overcome both those issues.

These breads are made using the normal ingredients you can find locally, so there's no need to have to order anything or have to go to any specialty stores for any of them. With these beads, you can enjoy the same meals you used to enjoy but stay on track with your diet as much as you want.

Whether you are starting the Keto diet yourself or looking for some healthy alternative to your traditional bread I'm sure you will find a recipe in this book that suits you. From savory to sweet, these recipes are not just satisfying but healthy too. And with the use of the bread machine, they take very little effort to make.

Lose the weight you want to lose, feel great, and still get to indulge in that piping hot piece of bread every now and then. Spread on your favorite topping and your bread craving will be satisfied.

Having one in your home will allow you to indulge in a wide array of Keto bread, cakes, and treats that are fresh and homemade. With this machine, you get to control the ingredient that you use, so you can use the ketogenic-approved food items. An appliance like this will support you on your journey toward the ketogenic lifestyle, weight loss, and healthy living in general.

Moreover, we have learned that the bread machine is a vital tool to have in our kitchen. It is actually not that hard to put into use. All you need to learn is how it functions and what its features are. You also need to use it more often in order to learn the dos and don'ts of using the machine.

It is only through practice that you will get more confidence and experience in using this machine. The bread machine comes with a set of instructions that you must learn from the manual in order to use it the right way. There is a certain way of loading the ingredients that must be followed, and the instructions vary according to the make and the model. So, when you first get a machine, sit down and learn the manual from start to finish; this allows you to put it to good use and get better results. The manual will tell you exactly what to put in it, as well as the correct settings to use, according to the different recipes and the type of bread you want to make.

FRIENDSHIP

IS THE

BREAD

OF THE HEART

M. R. MITFORD

CPSIA information can be obtained
at www.ICGtesting.com
Printed in the USA
BVHW021522130621
609469BV00005B/451